This journal belongs to:

The Animal Legacies Journal

Welcome to this powerful journal! This journal was inspired by the anthology *The Animal Legacies*. Our desire in creating this journal is to provide you a tool to support you in connecting further with animals, understanding the impact they have in your life, and receiving the powerful messages from their hearts to your heart.

In these pages, you'll find room to explore and capture your thoughts, reflections, and ideas and hear the messages your heart and spirit are wanting to share with you. On the front outside corner of each page, you will see a graphic reminding you of the love animals have for you and the imprint they are leaving in your life. We left the back of each page blank so you can capture pictures, images, and/or visual messages that don't fit as well within the lines on the front of each page.

I encourage you to take some time each day to stop, pause, and listen to what is being spoken into your heart and spirit and give yourself the opportunity to bring this powerful information and insight forward by writing it out. We left you lots of open lines and room to capture your thoughts and insights.

For those of you who like to have something to respond to or write about, we also wanted to give you some possible reflection points and tips to support you.

1. **We would encourage you to buy a copy of *The Animal Legacies*, an anthology compiled by Rebecca Hall Gruyter.** (This powerful book has great tips, deep and powerful shares by multiple experts coming together to share powerful messages they have received from animals and have been led to share from their hearts to your heart.)

2. **We encourage you to consider the following Reflection Points:**

    a. What gift, skill, activity, or way of being are you discovering about yourself?

    b. What message(s) are animals in your life sharing with you?

c. What message(s) is on your heart to share with animals in your life?

   d. How can you use this discovery about yourself to step or move forward in areas of your life that are most important to you?

   e. Where are you feeling blocked? And how can you possibly move through or around the block?

   f. What areas in life are most important to you?

   g. How can you share more of yourself?

   h. Where have you been hiding?

   i. How can you bring more of your gifts forward?

   j. What three things are you celebrating doing, being, seeing, and/or receiving today?

3. **Tap into another part of yourself activity.** Write a question with your dominant hand (the hand you normally use to write). Then put your pen/pencil in your other hand (your non-dominant hand, the one opposite to the hand you normally write with) and write a response/answer to the question. This taps into the opposite side of the brain than you normally go to for answers and information when writing. You will find great insight and wisdom by accessing more of yourself, especially parts of your mind you aren't always going to for information and insights. Remember, handwriting doesn't count. Feel and receive this powerful information and insight by tapping into more of yourself…and listening and receiving.

4. **Listen to music that helps you pause, reflect, and be present to your thoughts.** Take several breaths to center yourself. Perhaps light a candle to represent lighting your brilliance and sharing it with the world. Then take 5-10 minutes to write what comes to your heart and spirit…not analyzing…just writing and seeing what your heart and spirit have to say to you today.

5. **Remember: animals are a gift and absolutely needed in this world. How are they showing up as a gift in your life?** Here are some additional reflection points for you to consider on those days you are looking for some writing prompts to get you started. Be willing to take time to celebrate the gift of yourself and of life and be willing to share the gift of yourself with others. In light of this, write a response to the following questions:

    a. What is your animal thought for the day (what is an animal reminding you of today)?

    b. What action are you going to take today based on this information?

    c. What insight/idea/suggestion/reminder are you BEing?

    d. What animal experience are you celebrating today?

The next step is yours. Drink in the insights and wisdom that animals are sharing with you that support and inspire you. Take the time to pause, read, and reflect. Listen to the powerful messages of love that animals are sharing with you. I invite you to lean in and truly receive the messages and wisdom that will speak to your heart and soul.

-----Rebecca Hall Gruyter, Global Influencer

Founder/Owner of Your Purpose Driven Practice and CEO of RHG Media Productions

Closing Thoughts

I hope you have been touched by this journal and it has provided you a powerful time of connection and reflection. Listed below, please find tools, books (available on Amazon), and resources that can further support you on stepping further and further into your brilliance and sharing it out powerfully, as we believe what the world needs is more of you. We can't wait to see you, hear from you, and celebrate you as you share the gift of yourself with the world! *May you choose to listen to your powerful animal friends and be uplifted, encouraged, and empowered to SHINE!*

****

Books compiled or written by Rebecca Hall Gruyter to be released in 2020:

The Expert and Influencers Series: Women's Empowerment Edition

This powerful anthology will feature up to 30 experts and influencers committed to informing and uplifting you in the area of Women's Empowerment. From their personal and professional leadership experiences, each author will share tips, advice, and powerful insights to help you step forward as a leader in your life and business. (To be released June 2020).

Step Into Your Mission and Purpose!

This book, the second in our *Step Into* anthology series, takes the reader through the next step in their journey to SHINE! Featuring up to 30 authors, this anthology empowers readers to embrace their brilliance and choice so they can discover their unique mission and purpose in life. You will learn what it means to make the choice to live your life on purpose and with purpose. Each chapter, though the wisdom of this selection of authors, will empower and equip you to develop your own practice of living your purpose every day. Because the world needs you and your brilliance! (To be released 2021).

Bloom and SHINE!

This 365 daily inspiration book is designed to walk beside you each and every day of the year, giving you encouragement, wisdom, and insightful tips to help you bloom and shine each and every day of the year! (To be released in October 2020)

Anthologies compiled by Rebecca Hall Gruyter that are available now:

SHINE Series (Compiled and led by Rebecca Hall Gruyter)

Come out of Hiding and SHINE! (Book 1 in the SHINE Series)

Bloom Where You are Planted and SHINE! (Book 2 in the SHINE Series)

Step Forward and SHINE! (Book 3 and final book in the SHINE Series)

Step Into Series (Compiled and led by Rebecca Hall Gruyter)

Step Into Your Brilliance! (2019, Book 1 in the Step Into Series)

Step Into Your Mission & Purpose! (2021, Book 2 in the Step Into Series)

Experts & Influencers Series (Compiled and led by Rebecca Hall Gruyter)

Experts & Influencers Series: Leadership (2019, Book 1 in the Experts & Influencers Series)

Experts & Influencers Series: Women's Empowerment (2020, Book 2 in the Experts & Influencers Series)

Experts & Influencers Series: Speakers (2021, Book 3 in the Experts & Influencers Series)

The Grandmother Legacies (Anthology compiled by Rebecca Hall Gruyter)

Empowering YOU, Transforming Lives (365 Daily Inspiration Anthology compiled by Rebecca Hall Gruyter)

Books featuring a chapter by Rebecca Hall Gruyter that are available now:

The 40/40 Rules Anthology compiled by Holly Porter

Becoming Outrageously Successful Anthology compiled by Dr. Anita Jackson

Catch Your Star Anthology published by THRIVE Publishing

Discover Your Destiny Anthology compiled by Denise Joy Thompson

Gateway to An Enlightened World: Collective Lessons on Personal Transformation compiled by Dr. Ruth Anderson

I Am Beautiful Anthology compiled by Teresa Hawley-Howard

The Power of Our Voices, Sharing Our Story Anthology, compiled by Teresa Hawley-Howard

Real Estate Investing For Women Anthology compiled by Moneeka Sawyer

Succeeding Against All Odds Anthology compiled by Sandra Yancey

Success Secrets for Today's Feminine Entrepreneurs Anthology compiled by Dr. Anita Jackson

Unstoppable Woman of Purpose Anthology and workbook compiled by Nella Chikwe

Women on a Mission Anthology compiled by Teresa Hawley-Howard

Women of Courage, Women of Destiny Anthology compiled by Dr. Anita Jackson

Women Warriors Who Make It Rock Anthology compiled by Nichole Peters

You Are Whole, Perfect, and Complete - Just As You Are Anthology compiled by Carol Plummer and Susan Driscoll

Dear Powerful Reader,

Thank you for leaning into our journal. I hope it has encouraged and empowered and uplifted you.

I wanted to share a little bit more about our organizations, Your Purpose Driven Practice™, RHG TV Network™, RHG Publishing™, and RHG Media Productions™. We are passionate about helping others live on purpose and with purpose in their life and business. I hope this book has supported and inspired you to choose to live on purpose and with great purpose in your leadership!

If you are wanting to reach more people and be part of inspiring and supporting others with your message, your gifts, and the work that you bring to the world, then I want to share some opportunities for you to consider.

Each year we compile and produce anthology book projects, support authors in publishing their own powerful books as bestsellers, produce and publish an international magazine, launch TV shows, facilitate women's empowerment conferences, get quoted in major media, launch radio and podcast shows, and help experts and speakers step into a place of powerful influence to make a global difference. We provide programs and strategies to help you reach more people and facilitate the Speaker Talent Search (which helps speakers, experts, and influencers connect with more speaking opportunities). We would love to support you in reaching more people. Please take a moment to learn a little bit more about us at the sites listed below, and then reach out to us for a conversation. **We would love to help you be Seen, Heard, Have Impact, and SHINE!**

You can learn more about each of these things at our main website:
www.YourPurposeDrivenPractice.com

Enjoy our powerful **TV and podcast shows**:
www.RHGTVNetwork.com

Learn more about the **Speaker Talent Search™**:
www.SpeakerTalentSearch.com

Learn more about our **writing opportunities**: http://yourpurposedrivenpractice.com/writing-opportunities/

If you would like to connect with me personally to explore some of our opportunities in upcoming book projects, podcast/radio shows, and/or TV, then here is the link to schedule a time to speak with me directly: www.MeetWithRebecca.com, or you can email me at: Rebecca@YourPuposeDrivenPractice.com.

May you always choose to Be Seen, be Heard, Have Impact, and SHINE!

Warmly,

Rebecca Hall Gruyter

Rebecca Hall Gruyter is an Influencer and Empowerment Leader committed to bringing Experts and Influencers forward so that together we can lean in and make the world a better place one heart and life at a time. She is the owner of *Your Purpose Driven Practice*, creator of the *Women's Empowerment Series* events/TV show, the *Speaker Talent Search™*, and *Your Success Formula™*. Rebecca is an in-demand speaker, an expert money coach, and a frequent guest expert on success panels, tele-summits, TV shows, and radio shows. Rebecca specializes in using her promotional reach of over 10 million to help you be Seen, be Heard, and SHINE!

As the CEO of *RHG Media Productions™*, Rebecca launched the international TV Network www.RHGTVNetwork.com to bring even more positive and transformational programming to the world. In July 2017, she launched the Global RHG Magazine & TV Guide, bringing inspirational influences and their messages to the world! In January 2018, she expanded RHG Publishing to now help individual authors bring their books forward as bestsellers so they can be positioned as they bring their powerful book forward.

Rebecca is a popular and syndicated radio talk-show host, a #1 bestselling author (multiple times), and a publisher who wants to help YOU impact the world powerfully!

(925) 787-1572

Rebecca@YourPurposeDrivenPractice.com

www.facebook.com/rhallgruyter (Facebook)

www.YourPurposeDrivenPractice.com (Main website)

www.RHGTVNetwork.com (TV network)

www.SpeakerTalentSearch.com (Free opportunity for speakers to get on more stages)

www.EmpoweringWomenTransformingLives.com (Weekly radio show)

www.MeetWithRebecca.com (Calendar link to schedule a time to talk with Rebecca)

www.ingramcontent.com/pod-product-compliance
Lightning Source LLC
LaVergne TN
LVHW011725060526
838200LV00051B/3031